Legacy Letters
from
Your Heart

Beth LaMie

Copyright © 2016 by Beth LaMie

Published by
Little Duck Publishing
2620 W Anchorage Road NE
Solon, IA 52333

Cover design, book design and layout by Beth LaMie

ISBN 978-0-9840780-3-5

Printed in the United States of America

10 9 8 7 6 5 4 3 2

Table of Contents

PART ONE: OVERVIEW

Sharing What Matters...to You

A legacy letter is a simple way to share what is important to you with your family and friends. It is neither legal nor financial, but to your family it is priceless.

If you knew ahead of time your last day on earth, what words of wisdom and comfort would you want to leave your family? A legacy letter gives your loved ones a better understanding of who you are, as well as what is important to you, and what hopes you want to pass on to them.

It is a legacy of love and a spiritual gift for your loved ones to remember you now and for years to come.

Think about what you wish you knew about your parents, grandparents, and other ancestors. For example, why did your family uproot their lives to emigrate from one area of the country to another, such as the pioneers who endured hardships to settle the West? You can share relevant experiences with your own descendants and friends.

Many people think about writing a legacy letter when they are nearing the end of their life. In reality, such letters

1

would ideally be an ongoing practice, especially after high school.

Consider starting a legacy letter as soon as possible, regardless of your age. Update it regularly prior to or after major milestones, such as graduations, marriage and divorce, births and deaths, personal achievements, and world events. Reviewing each version can show how much you have changed and grown over the years.

Life is too short and too precious to miss the opportunity to leave a legacy letter to your family.

Start now!

Chapter One: What in the World Is a Legacy Letter?

Understanding Legacy Letters

*"The only thing
you take with you
when you're gone
is what you leave behind."*
~ John Allston

Death and taxes—the only two certainties in life. As we mature, we may grow concerned about leaving behind a legacy for our family, children, and future generations. Wanting to be remembered, we also want to give our loved ones the benefit of our experiences and wisdom. An excellent way to share that information is through a legacy letter to family and friends.

What Is a Legacy Letter?

Definition

A *legacy letter* is a document that shares significant thoughts with loved ones. It is also known as an *ethical will*. It is a non-legal document that passes on important information about you and your ancestors to your loved ones and descendants.

A *legacy letter*, also called an *ethical will*, is usually a written document created to share your significant thoughts with loved ones, such as personal values, experiences, wisdom, and blessings. It can be shared with family members or friends either when written, or preserved and shared after the author's death.

Ethical wills began as a Jewish tradition over 3,000 years ago. The initial practice passed down values orally to future generations. Topics typically included the family's lineage back to earliest times. Modern audiences find an updated approach appeals to their need to leave a similar legacy.

Whether a legacy letter or ethical will is as brief as a few paragraphs, or as long as a complete memoir, it contains a heartfelt and enduring communication that serves as a reminder of a person's love and caring. The majority of legacy letters are written, but other alternatives will be considered later in this book. When written by hand, the document becomes a lovely keepsake of an individual's distinctive handwriting.

Last Will vs. Living Will vs. Legacy Letter

> **Definition**
>
> A *last will* is a legal document that determines how your assets will be distributed after your death.

A *last will* handles the legal dissolution of financial matters, including property, money, and assets. In the event a last will doesn't exist at the time of death, you are intestate and the state of residence determines the distribution of the estate.

For all legal matters, such as creating a last will, it is important you seek appropriate counsel. It is especially important to prepare in advance if your family includes children or anyone with special needs.

> **Definition**
>
> A *living will* is a legal document that expresses your desires on whether to prolong your life in the event of a terminal condition.

A *living will* is a legal document that contains health directives for end-of-life situations. In the event you cannot express your own desires at that time, such as when in a coma, this document informs caregivers of your final wishes.

> **Definition**
>
> A *power of attorney* is a legal document that designates someone to make decisions on your behalf for financial or health care matters.

A *power of attorney* grants the right to a person you delegate to make decisions for you in the event you cannot make them. You can create separate powers of attorney for financial matters and for health care.

In contrast to the documents mentioned above, a legacy letter is neither a legal nor a financial document. However, to your family and loved ones, it is priceless. A legacy letter allows you to speak from the heart and leave an enduring legacy for your family and future generations. It makes an ideal addition to your estate planning.

Why Write a Legacy Letter?

The act of writing a legacy letter can affect you for the rest of your life. How? It provides an excellent way for you to look at your life as a whole. Will future generations remember who you are? Are you satisfied with your accomplishments? Have you left your mark in the world in some way that makes you proud? Do you feel your life has been worthwhile?

If the answer to any of these questions is "No," consider that now is the perfect time to reassess (or establish) your goals and life plan. It's not too late to align your life with your passions. As you complete your legacy letter, you have an opportunity to get your life on track.

Creating a legacy letter gives you the opportunity to:

- Examine who you are and who you want to be
- Preserve your family stories for the future
- Express your innermost thoughts and concerns
- Leave a lasting gift to loved ones
- Come to terms with your mortality
- Achieve a small sense of immortality

A legacy letter is one way

to find peace of mind

by leaving a piece of your mind

for your loved ones.

Who Benefits from a Legacy Letter?

The *primary beneficiary* of a legacy letter is you—the writer. It is all about you: your story, in your voice. As you examine your own life and heritage, you determine exactly what to include. You have the opportunity to preserve the life you've lived and envision your life yet to come.

The *secondary beneficiaries* of a legacy letter are the recipients. Whether you share the document upon completing it, or preserve it until after your death, your loved ones will receive an enduring reminder of you, your values, and what you consider important in life.

Recipients of your legacy letter can:

- Learn details about your ancestry and heritage
- Understand your outlook and innermost thoughts
- Feel comfort that you cared enough to leave a final communication
- Come to terms with losing a loved one, now or in the future
- Retain a lasting memory of you

When to Write a Legacy Letter

The best time to write a legacy letter is NOW! Not knowing how long you will live or retain your faculties, the sooner you start, the better. Legacy letters don't need to be perfect—there is no wrong way to create one. The important thing is to preserve whatever thoughts you want to share with your family and friends. You can always expand or modify your document at a later date.

Every five years or so, review the document and revise or update it as needed. One advantage of starting at an earlier rather than later age is having a chance to observe your own growth over the previous period. The analysis may also indicate if your life is proceeding in the direction you desire.

What's in a Legacy Letter?

The content of a legacy letter is up to you. It can be as

short as a paragraph or two, as long as a book, or more likely somewhere in between. Samples in Appendix B give you a better idea about how simple and straight-forward they can be.

Which portions are the most important to leave in your legacy? They may include your personal values, ethics, religion, memories, heritage, or family stories. By design, these topics may all become elements of a legacy letter.

The main concept to remember is that your legacy letter is uniquely yours. No two are alike. Speak from your heart and tell your dear friends and descendants about yourself and your family. Stories are a wonderful way to share cherished life memories.

Potential Components of a Legacy Letter

- Opening
- Personal Values and Beliefs
- Your History—Past and Present
- Lessons from Life Experiences
- Hopes for the Future
- Closing

In the following chapters, you will learn more details about the content of a legacy letter. However, you will determine precisely which of the above elements you want to include.

Legacy Letters from Your Heart

♥

PART TWO: POTENTIAL COMPONENTS OF A LEGACY LETTER

All the Necessary Pieces

♥

Chapter Two: Opening Your Legacy Letter

Dear _____, or To My Beloved Descendants

*"The way to get started is to quit
talking and begin doing."*
~ Walt Disney

You may want to address your legacy letter to one particular person to help you stay focused. Completing your first legacy letter, such as for your husband, makes it much easier to write a separate version for your children or friends; simply modify the original letter by removing or adding relevant passages and stories for each person. That way, you can customize each letter to apply to specific individuals as you desire.

To open your legacy letter, choose one of the following sample salutations or something that feels comfortable to you.

- *To the most important person (people) in my life...*
- *To my loving family, these words are the legacy of love I leave you.*

- *Dear _____, [husband, wife, children, grandchildren, etc.] I want you to know what I learned in my life.*
- *A letter for my future generations.*
- *Dearest Children: A few words to explain the distribution of my assets.*

FIRST DRAFT ABOUT MY OPENING:

_____

_____

_____

_____

_____

_____

_____

_____

_____

_____

_____

_____

_____

_____

_____

_____

Chapter Three: Personal Values and Beliefs

Treasures from Your Heart: Values over Valuables

*"It's not hard to make decisions
when you know what your values are."*
~ Roy Disney

What Are Personal Values?

> **Definition**
>
> *Personal values* are our convictions and principles about what is right and wrong, good and bad, desirable and undesirable.

Personal values enable us to live in a way that allows us to be true to ourselves. Together, they form a specific code of conduct regarding what is important for each of us. In fact, they govern what we need to be happy and content.

Values vary from person to person and perhaps they vary even for one person from time to time. They explain what is important to us, what we will not compromise, and what we hold dear. When we don't honor our personal values, we experience internal conflict and stress.

15

Early in life, each person begins to form their own personal values and beliefs based on ideals demonstrated at home. As people mature, their beliefs evolve as the result of interaction with family, friends, neighbors, peers, teachers, religious leaders, and others.

Why Are They Important?

Personal values form your character and determine how you respond in certain situations. For example, if a cashier hands you too much change, will you pocket it and walk away, or will you hand it back? If you keep it, will you regret it later? Would you act differently if your child is watching you?

Values make you more aware of what you intrinsically believe is right or wrong. When you act against that instinct, your conscience will likely bother you. Honoring your values helps to maintain your internal peace.

Values over Valuables

During an economic downturn, individuals may realize their financial situation prohibits leaving a substantial inheritance to their children and heirs. Fortunately, a recent survey discovered baby boomers prefer a *nonfinancial inheritance* from their parents.

Allianz Life Insurance Company of North America conducted a survey of over 2600 baby boomers and elders. According to the results, participants felt a non-financial legacy was *ten times more important than money and other assets*. The response overwhelmingly favored a personal heritage over worldly goods. In other words, they preferred values over valuables.

Seventy-seven percent of boomers and elders personally felt values and life experiences were very important parts of an inheritance. How exciting to realize that virtually every single person has the ability to leave a meaningful heritage!

Which types of values are the most important to leave as a legacy? They include personal values, ethics, religion, memories, heritage, and family stories. Not coincidentally, these concepts can all become elements of a legacy letter.

Exercise #1 – Identifying Your Personal Values

This exercise will help you start thinking about your own personal values and those of the people around you. You may begin to notice similarities and discrepancies as you pay attention to the values of close friends, casual acquaintances, and even individuals in the news. As you might expect, we tend to feel most comfortable with others who have comparable ideals.

Look at the list of sample values below. Which ones can you relate to the most? On the left side of the words, mark at least three beliefs. Feel free to add more values to the list in the blank spaces at the bottom, or create your own group of words.

SAMPLE VALUES

activism	authenticity	charity
chivalry	communication	compassion
confidence	courage	creativity
curiosity	dignity	diversity
empathy	endurance	enthusiasm
excitement	fairness	faith
friendship	God	gratitude
hard work	helpfulness	honesty
honor	hope	humility
independence	integrity	interest
inventiveness	joyfulness	kindness
learning	listening	love
loyalty	motivation	nonviolence
open mindedness	organization	patience
persistence	positive attitude	pride (not ego)
promptness	quality	religion
resourcefulness	respect	responsibility

self-esteem	sense of humor	service
support	tolerance	tradition
vivacity	wisdom	work ethic

One of the interesting benefits of this particular exercise is the opportunity to expand on your own list of personal values. As you look over the sample values above, you may notice some principles that appeal to you. This is the perfect time to consider which of them you want to actively pursue. For example, in your youth, you may have toyed with the idea of joining the circus to work with wild animals, but never followed up on it.

Now that you are more mature, you may find ways to realize that dream in some way. A few options could be to work as a volunteer at an animal preserve, raise money for a wildlife group, or spend a vacation tracking bottle-nose dolphin during an ongoing Elderhostel study in Belize. Creating your legacy letter allows you to look at your life and decide what has been important, as well as what is important for the remaining years of your life.

Excerpt from a sample legacy letter from a mother of two young boys:

In my own journey some of the other things that I have come to value [is] the following:

Gratitude: There is a beautiful verse from the New

Testament, "In everything, give thanks," and I think that in every situation in life, giving thanks for the good that exists—despite the hardships—is a valuable mindset. I have also learned that hardships can teach important lessons when I have been willing to learn. This isn't to say that I have been grateful for the hardship itself, but that I tried to have a mindset that looks for the good in every situation. [...]

Exercise #2 – Understanding Your Personal Values

Once you select a few values in the first exercise, think about and answer the questions below. Keep in mind there are no wrong answers, since each person's values will be uniquely theirs. This exercise may take a little while, as you think back to when you grew up, where you've been, and where you are going. If you need more space to write, just use any paper (or the writing journal we'll discuss in Chapter 10) and write as much as you desire.

1. Which values are most important to you? Why?

2. From whom did you learn these values? How?

3. Which values do you want to see in others around you? Why?

4. In what ways do you act on your values? Describe specific examples.

5. Do your values help you make difficult decisions? Why or why not?

6. What is the best example you have seen of values in action? How did seeing it affect you?

FIRST DRAFT ABOUT MY PERSONAL VALUES AND BELIEFS

Chapter Four: Your History – Past and Present

Heritage, History, and Splitting Heirs

"In all of us there is a hunger, marrow-deep, to know our heritage, to know who we are and where we came from."
~ Alex Haley

The Importance of Preserving Stories

Every person has a story to tell, and so does every family. When elderly members pass away, essential tales and knowledge disappear forever. Sadly, people often do not recognize that sense of urgency until too late. The sooner you act to preserve those stories, the more complete you can make your legacy.

By including your family's history in a legacy letter, you create a collection of priceless gifts to current and future generations: 1) the preservation of a portion of your heritage, consisting of your family stories, customs, and traditions; 2) a piece *of yourself*, by taking the time and making the effort to keep precious stories alive forever; and 3) a gift *for yourself*. Learning more information about your family gives you an excellent opportunity to know and appreciate who you are, perhaps the most precious gift of all.

Stories from Your Ancestors

Think about all the colorful stories you heard over the years from or about your ancestors. You need to include that heritage in a legacy letter for your loved ones, now and for the future. Consider which stories best explain the essence of your family's spirit, adventures, hereditary traits, and history.

If needed, find out more details about specific events, such as what prompted them to pursue a certain career or calling, why they emigrated from another country, or how they survived a catastrophic event. Your research may include interviews with family members and friends, as well as historical records and genealogies. Relatives often pass down a combination of facts, legends, and folklore over several generations. Those stories can greatly enhance your legacy letter.

Even if you have little or no knowledge of your elders, and no one else remembers them either, you may discover helpful, factual information in public records, newspapers, and archives. With a few details and a bit of luck, you can search online databases that contain a vast amount of material from census records, cemeteries and churches, and military documents.

You can perform much of the research yourself, with the

aid of genealogical data, such as that available at www.ancestry.com. Libraries, history museums, and genealogy groups offer a variety of tools. If you don't have the time or the inclination to delve into such minutiae, enlist family members to assist in the study. In addition, professional resources can help in your fact-finding mission, such as the Association of Personal Historians, www.personalhistorians.org, and the National Genealogical Society, www.ngsgenealogy.org.

Understanding your heritage gives your loved ones a keen sense of family traits passed down to their generation, both good and bad. You never know what to expect from your investigation. But whether it turns out uplifting, inspirational, disappointing, or even shocking, knowledge is power—share it with others.

When you realize some of the trials and tribulations your ancestors survived, you gain a true sense of how heredity helped form your character. In fact, you may discover you flourish either because of or in spite of previous generations.

Exercise #1 — Exploring Your Heritage

Consider the following questions with regard to their importance to you and your family as a whole. Make notes below or in your writing journal about events you want to explore further, along with potential ways you can dig into the details.

Questions to explore about physical locations

1. How did you or your ancestors decide to live in a particular area? What motivated them to move from one location to another?

2. Did you or your predecessors emigrate from another country? If so, what did you/they want to find or avoid? How successfully did it turn out?

3. If you descended from cultures, ethnicities, or groups that endured prejudice, what experiences did you or your ancestors have and how did you/they survive?

4. Did you or your forefathers suffer hardships and/or triumphs due to wars, fighting, unrest, or other upheavals? How did you/they overcome the challenges?

5. Do/did previous generations live within a specific region, or did they spread out to other areas, states, or countries? Who made the decisions about where to live and why?

Questions to explore about acts of heroism, patriotism, and courage

1. What events in your family's history demonstrate admirable qualities, such as patriotism during war, heroism after 9/11, or courage in difficult situations? How did such acts affect other people, both at the time and in the long run?

2. Did you or your family participate in momentous events, such as the Revolutionary War, Women's Suffrage, Prohibition, the Civil Rights Movement, or others? What impact did it have on you/them?

3. What examples in your lineage pointed to unusual careers or occupations? For example, Pony Express rider, gold miner, hangman, hot air balloonist, junk man, war code breaker, explorer, or inventor? When you dug into your family's history, did the results surprise, delight, or appall you?

Questions to explore about family heirlooms and traits

1. Have any heirlooms passed down through your family, such as jewelry, souvenirs, furniture, documents, mementos, or articles of clothing? What do they represent in terms of importance to you and your family? Who brought them into your clan and under what circumstances?

2. What similar traits exist among your family members, such as a distinctive receding hairline, birthmark, webbed toes, manner of speaking, or specific frown lines? How far back can you trace them?

3. Which, if any, family recipes contained secret ingredients revealed only upon swearing to never divulge them? Did your family preserve the tradition for generations, or did someone give up the ghost?

Stories from Your Life

Your own experiences form crucial elements of your legacy letter. Drawing from personal knowledge enables you to share examples of how you survived tough times, which people and outside factors impacted your life, and what you hope future generations can learn from your triumphs and failures.

Stories don't have to be exciting to maintain interest. Writing about events from a normal day can make a charming story for a person who hasn't experienced the same things. In addition, someone familiar with the actual facts will also enjoy reading about your recollections. When people read your stories, they may experience something new by seeing it through your eyes.

As you consider all the stories about your life, reflect on which of them best portray what you want future generations to remember about you. Whether you decide to share the precise details of a legendary tale exaggerated over the years, or reveal previously unknown information about yourself, the decision rests with you. After all, a legacy letter represents your personal legacy to family and loved ones.

Exercise #2 — Exploring Your Experiences

Write down a few significant memories in the spaces below or in your writing journal. Don't worry about sentence structure or punctuation. Consider times and

29

events from your own personal history, or your ancestor's, and explain the importance.

Use this exercise to brush away a few cobwebs so you can recall details from the past. Spend some time reminiscing with close friends or elders as you look through old photograph albums. You may discover long-forgotten events with cherished love ones. Enjoy this process of rooting out those memories close to your heart.

For additional ideas on how to gather memories from your past, please see Chapter 9.

Earliest Memories	Homes You Lived In
Childhood or Growing Up Years	Marriage or No Marriage
Teenage Years	Becoming a Parent or Not
Adult Years	Being a Grandparent or Not
Memorable "Firsts," First Kiss, First Car, First Apartment, etc.	Family Heirlooms and Heritage
Mentors and Mentoring	Education and Career Choices

Milestones from History	Military Service

Telling the Tall Tales

What information do you want to ensure your family knows about you and your ancestors? When you start writing stories, such as in your legacy letter, write about what you already know. Include stories about things you experienced or heard about from family members.

Sometimes, certain tales become embellished over years of retelling, until they stray far from the original truth. How you handle less-than-accurate renditions of your family stories remains up to you. You may choose to relate them just as you heard, which entertains others, or you may decide to stick with the more factual albeit less enjoyable versions. Again, you make the choice.

Example:

A woman in one of my writing workshops worried about how to relay legendary stories her deceased father told. He stopped just shy of completely fanciful fiction, on the scale of how Paul Bunyan and Babe the Blue Ox dug the Grand Canyon. But she loved his stories and his expressive presentations.

I suggested she tell the stories just as he told them to her, with flair and panache. She could also mention how much she enjoyed his active imagination, even though he tended to exaggerate. The most important aspect for her? She wanted to capture the essence of how much she enjoyed his captivating stories.

Excerpt from a sample legacy letter from a grandmother of nine:

Be proud of our ancestors who knew the value of a hard day's work. We come from strong stock of farmers, laborers, shopkeepers, and people unafraid to reach for the American dream to own a home. Although many of them had minimal education, they understood the power of learning as much as they could. They sacrificed so that we could have more than they did.

FIRST DRAFT ABOUT MY HISTORY – PAST AND PRESENT:

♥

Chapter Five: Learning from Life Experiences

Do As I Say, Not as I Did

"The major value in life is not what you get.
The major value in life is what you become."
  ~ Jim Rohn

All of us have hopes and dreams—for ourselves, for other people, and for the world. A legacy letter is the perfect venue to encourage writers to share those positive thoughts for the future with their loved ones.

Life Lessons and Achievements

A - Life Lessons

What have you learned during your life, when, and how? Your life lessons often shape who you are and who you become. Everyone experiences and responds differently to life lessons. That is why they are such an important element of your legacy letter. Share the details of your significant experiences.

It is important for children, young adults, and others to realize that your life was not a bed of roses. In spite of difficult times, you somehow moved forward and made the best of it. They need to understand that one misstep or setback (or even a series of them) does not have to condemn them; it simply means they need to work harder to overcome the situation.

- *I learned this from my father: find something you love to do, work hard, and be proud of yourself; only later did other people say girls aren't "supposed" to compete with boys. I proved they were wrong.*
- *My mother provided the inspiration to be the best I could be and to never give up on my dreams.*
- *Playing chess taught me to plan ahead, be patient, and anticipate the desired outcome.*
- *My grandmother showed me how to be a lady and still get what I wanted; behind every successful man is a strong woman.*

B – Growth from Losses and Failures

No one has a perfect life. There are trials and tribulations, heartbreaks, disappointments, tragedies, losses, and failures. Ideally, they become opportunities for reflection and growth.

Think about your challenges and the impact they had on your development. Did you go under at first? Did you eventually overcome? Did you gain compassion, patience, or greater understanding? Maybe even wisdom? Were you bitter? Were you able to forgive others? Yourself?

This is difficult material to visit but worthwhile. While your legacy letter will hopefully be positive and encouraging, you do not want it to become an impossibly perfect life without substance and depth. Thoughtfully share both the good and the bad.

- *When I lost my job [scholarship, love of my life, etc.], I discovered that...*
- *My illness [or losing my legs] taught me the importance of...*
- *My divorce(s) proved to me...*
- *The tragedy of my childhood enabled me to...*
- *I regret that I didn't learn sooner to...*

C - Achievements and Accomplishments

What have been your proudest accomplishments and why? What can your descendants learn from your successes and missteps? Which achievements by your family have made you proud? How does having confidence in yourself lead you to more successes?

- *My greatest achievement has been...[such as: overcoming certain challenges, publishing a book that helps people communicate better, going back to school, becoming a certified Scuba Diver, sacrificing for my own or my children's education, working with troubled teens, etc.]*
- *I am proud of the way my family [son, daughter, grandchildren, etc.] has...*
- *In spite of a troubled youth, my son [daughter, uncle, friend, etc.] was able to...*

D - Gratitude

What are you grateful for and why? Focus on the good things in your life, even amid challenges.

- *I am grateful for ... a warm bed ... a loving, supportive family ... and great friends.*

- *I cherish beauty in nature.*
- *I appreciate opportunities to grow and learn.*
- *I am blessed to live in a country that allows freedom of speech and religion.*
- *I am fortunate to have been born with a few innate talents that led me to ...*

E - Advice

What advice do you want your friends and family to remember? Flesh out your advice with stories and examples. How can you help them in some way? Think about the wisdom you can bequeath to them. What are your favorite poems, quotes, books, and why?

- *Always treat others as you want to be treated.*
- *A bird in the hand is worth two in the bush.*
- *Look for the good in people.*
- *Don't do anything you want to hide from your mother [father, grandchildren, etc.].*
- *Follow your dreams.*
- *Do something good for people, every day, whenever possible.*

FIRST DRAFT ABOUT MY LESSONS FROM LIFE EXPERIENCES

♥

Chapter Six: Hopes for the Future

Hopes, Dreams, and Happily Ever After

*"Hope gets us started; encouragement
keeps us going."*
~ Zig Ziglar

This chapter addresses your best future wishes, thoughts, and desires not only for your heirs, but also for yourself and for the world at large. It is a splendid way to bequeath your wisdom to others and to offer encouragement going forward.

Your powers of observation may offer you clues about what to include here for specific people. For example, you may have noticed that your young grandson has an enquiring mind when he frequently asks relevant questions about how things work and why; with his interest in mathematics and science, he might enjoy a career in engineering or computer sciences and your encouragement can help him pursuit a related field.

You may also have noticed skills in others that might lead to a satisfying vocation, such as a special way of handling difficult children, a comforting touch with the elderly, or a creative way of decorating. Sometimes people are not aware of their own talents, so it can be a blessing for you to point them out. Remember, if you find something you love to do, you will never work a day in your life.

What advice do you want to leave for youngsters? Can you offer suggestions as they grow up, such as how to find their soul mate or special love, how to keep and nurture that love, or how to stay calm in the midst of chaos? Take advantage of this opportunity to leave some words of wisdom.

Think about the hobbies and activities you enjoy; when you share the pleasure you have derived from them, you may discover a kindred spirit among your friends and family members. You might find satisfaction in teaching some of them about your knowledge of gardening, photography, painting, music, travel, quilting, woodworking, or any number of pleasant pastimes.

Consider your hopes for the future for yourself. Do you plan to travel, write a book, take a few classes, visit old friends in faraway places, perform charity work, see the Seven Wonders of the World, learn to play an instrument, or enter a national baking contest? Whatever these hopes are, share them with your loved ones. You may entice a companion to join in your upcoming adventures.

Reflect on what can make the world a better place, whether it is world peace, the end of war and hunger, a cure for cancer, or more kindness between strangers. Even if you cannot witness such lofty goals, you can certainly envision them. Share your vision with others. If they can help take one small step toward resolving such issues, humanity will certainly benefit.

Here are a few thought generators to get started:

My hopes and dreams for you…	Continue/create family traditions…
You have a special quality to…	May your friends and family…
Help others by…	I hope you find work that…
Follow the teachings of…	I want the world to…
May your days be…	Find peace with…

FIRST DRAFT ABOUT MY HOPES FOR THE FUTURE:

Chapter Seven: Closing Your Legacy Letter

Sealed with a Kiss...or Not

"Begin with the end in mind."
  ~ Stephen Covey

Having learned all the steps to consider when creating your legacy letter, use the closing to wrap up your final message. This last section covers your intention in preparing your final words to your family; it may include such things as a brief summary, expressions of love, and final wishes. Try to end on a positive note.

Decide on the closing message you want to use. It can be thought-provoking, amusing, serious, or whatever tone you choose; strive to instill a sense of hope and love for your family.

Here are some suggestions to close your legacy letter:
- *I love each of you with all my heart.*
- *Thank you for all the wonderful memories.*
- *Think of me when ...*
- *Don't do anything I wouldn't do, which leaves a lot of room.*
- *Remember me as you ...*

FIRST DRAFT ABOUT MY CLOSING:

PART THREE: MAKING YOUR LEGACY LETTER PERSONAL

How to Get It in Writing

♥

Chapter Eight: Handling Difficult Situations

The Good, the Bad, and the Ugly

*"All sorrows can be borne if you put them
into a story or tell a story about them."*
~ Isak Dinesen, Danish author

Every life is full of ups and downs, positive and negative, good and bad. Some of those occurrences are important factors in developing character. This chapter provides insight on how to handle delicate situations, such as personal challenges, failures, regrets, tragedies, and disappointments. In addition, various experiences may provide opportunities for individual growth.

During one of my recent memoir writing classes, I asked my students to close their eyes and think about a personal story that resonated with them, a story that clambered to be written, perhaps the reason they signed up for the class. After working just a few minutes, one woman had tears streaming down her cheeks. For privacy, we'll call her Bonnie.

As her tears continued, Bonnie spoke haltingly about a personal tragedy in her early youth. She struggled because she didn't know how to write about it. She felt torn between revealing the truth to her grown daughter and opening old wounds that had scarred over.

After further discussion in private, I suggested Bonnie perform a brain dump and write everything she remembered and felt about the incident, with no limitations, censorship, or editing. Afterward, she could decide exactly how much of that painful story to include in her memoir.

At our class the following week, Bonnie related how she spent hours writing, crying, and writing some more. In her first draft, she wrote almost twelve pages filled with pain, anger, and uncensored emotions. Rather than reading aloud everything that she had written, I suggested she choose a smaller portion of the story that she felt comfortable sharing with the group. As always in my classes, students have the option to read selectively or not at all, although everyone usually shares.

Writing that story proved to be both exhausting and cathartic. When Bonnie finished her tale, she felt relieved and at peace. From the original twelve pages, she condensed the essence of the story down to just a few paragraphs. That method worked out well for her. Bonnie needed her daughter to hear about what happened, but she didn't need to pass on all the brutal details.

So my advice when dealing with a difficult situation is to write it all out, then decide later exactly how much, if any, you want to share with select individuals.

Something else to keep in mind is that if you become emotionally drained or depressed after writing a particular story, consider finding someone to talk to, whether it be a close friend or family member, a psychologist or therapist, or a priest, minister, or rabbi. They can help you move forward after you've scraped your emotions raw.

Please don't be afraid to seek the help you may need.

♥

Chapter Nine: Story Starters to Get You Primed

Ferreting Out the Facts and Fallacies of Family Lore and Legends

"There was never yet an uninteresting life.
Such a thing is an impossibility.
Inside the dullest exterior,
there is a drama, a comedy, and a tragedy."
~ Mark Twain

When it comes to gathering personal stories, some writers find themselves staring at a blank page. Based on writing workshops delivered over the last several years, I've learned to use various prompts to help dig out precious memories and transform them into stories within a legacy letter.

Write About Your Own Life

When you start to write, it is easiest to write about what you already know. The older you are, the more stories you can draw from. You can tell stories about things that you have experienced yourself. What is your favorite or most vivid memory? Is it your first day at school, an outing with someone special, or the day you got married? Is it about watching fire engines race to a house in your neighborhood, winning a prize at the fair, or the trials of babysitting your little brother?

Think about the stories you enjoy reading. Notice that the author starts with an idea, such as a day at the lake and builds the story piece by piece. Was the weather warm and sunny, or cool and windy? Who are the people in the story? Can you picture what they looked like from the writer's descriptions? Did they roast hot dogs and marshmallows or enjoy cold chicken and Grandma's famous potato salad? Spicing up your stories with some colorful details provides fun reading.

Use the questions and suggestions in this book to dig out your own memories. Those are the first family stories you can preserve. The wealth of material you remember may surprise you once you start writing.

Stories All Around You

Stories don't have to be exciting to be interesting. Writing about things that happen on a normal day can make a charming tale for a person who hasn't experienced the same thing. In fact, even someone who is familiar with the actual events will enjoy reading about it. When people read your stories, they may experience something new by seeing it through your eyes.

For example, do you remember your first day of school?

How did you get there? Did you walk, take the bus, or ride in a car? Were you excited or maybe a little bit scared? Did you know other children in your class, or were they all strangers? What did you wear? Did you bring a brown bag lunch, or did you eat in a cafeteria at school? All of these details are things that people like to read about.

Getting the Younger Generation Involved

You can involve your grandchildren and youngsters of all ages in family stories by writing about your shared adventures. Jot down a few lines and ask them for input, which will vary depending on their ages. They may recall details that made less of an impression on you. For example, on a trip to the Children's Museum, my grandson was more thrilled about finding a fuzzy caterpillar in a corner than the actual museum. Capture their memories along with yours for truly personal family stories.

If your grandkids are still young, now is an excellent time to help record memories for them—a brief story and perhaps photos will help them recall it later. In fact, this is a great exercise for any family members who live far away from each other: have them take digital photos to send to each other with a short story about what they are doing. Even children as young as five can use a simple digital camera, but they may need help loading the images to a computer.

Using Milestone Events

There are memories from certain ages that offer us a wealth of stories to capture. Consider writing about what you remember from when you were sixteen years old and struggled to learn to drive, or the year you turned twenty-one, forty, sixty-five, or ninety. Each of these years is a potential milestone for you. Think about which of these years made the biggest impression on you and for what reason. Then you can develop each of those thoughts into a powerful story about how you felt and what meant the most to you.

You can also stimulate your recollections when you look at some of your "firsts" for important personal stories. Think about your first bicycle, your first night away from home, your first love, your first kiss, your first car, your first airplane ride or getting your first job. Whichever story tugs at your heart is where you should start looking for ideas.

Which Stories?

Think about it. You have dozens and dozens of interesting stories in your life. Consider the tales you like to tell your friends and family. Other people will be interested in reading them as well. You'll have an endless source of stories when you draw from the huge base of what you do and see every day.

When you get an idea for a story, start writing it as soon as you can. Don't worry about cleaning it up while you write. Otherwise, you may forget a really great idea. If you happen to lose the thread to the story, try coming back to it a little later.

♥

Chapter Ten: Writing Basics

Get Ready, Get Set, Get Writing!

*"Believe you can and
you're halfway there."*
~ Theodore Roosevelt

Many people are reluctant to write. Some may spell poorly, have few grammar skills, or lack confidence in how to construct a paragraph. Writing personal stories that are interesting to read can be a fun challenge. Grab readers with powerful descriptions, sensory words, and a lasting connection to favorite tales and folklore.

Do you remember years ago when you made a toy house with wooden building blocks? If so, then you know you started first with the floor, consequently followed by the walls and then the roof. Building a biography or autobiography is kind of the same. You can just start with a few simple writing guidelines and paragraph structure to create the story.

Basic Writing Guidelines

Every writer uses roughly the same steps. Sometimes you may be able to combine steps together. But stories will make more sense if you generally follow these basic writing guidelines.

1. **Brainstorming** – write down a bunch of ideas.
   - Don't judge if ideas are good or bad, just write them.
   - Get more ideas by talking to other people.
   - One idea leads to another until you get an idea you like.

2. **Rough Draft** – get your ideas down on paper.
   - Don't worry about grammar, spelling, or punctuation.
   - Write down ideas as fast as you can.
   - If one thought takes you in another direction, go with it.

3. **Revisions** – make the story flow.
   - Make sure each paragraph has a beginning, middle and ending.
   - Does the first paragraph make a nice lead into the rest of the story?
   - Are the paragraphs in sequence?
   - Is it interesting? Does it make sense to the reader?

4. **Editing** – fine-tune the story.
   - Clean up any grammar, spelling, and punctuation problems.
   - Add some pictures or your own drawings, if

you like.

- Read the story to someone else to get more ideas.

5. **Publishing** – print a copy of your story.
    - Print by computer or write it neatly by hand.
    - Read it to yourself or to a few people.
    - Listen to feedback and consider any changes.

Repeat any or all of the above steps until you feel comfortable with the story.

When you first start writing your family stories, using the above steps in order will help you stay on track. If you find one of the steps too difficult, then think about going back a step to revise what you have done so far.

At some point when you write a story, you may be able to start with brainstorming and move right through each of the first four steps. Almost all writers need to revise their work until they get it just right. It takes some hard work to make your story as good as you can, but having a story people want to read makes it all worthwhile.

The important thing is that you can revise, edit, modify, and perfect anything you write. After some time, you may want to pick up the thread of a given story and use it in other ways and other places. As the writer, you always have those options. The story belongs to you to discard or resurrect as you see fit.

Story Structure

The paragraph structure you use can also make a difference in the readability of your stories. Start out with a bang—grab your reader's attention so they want to read further. Use descriptive words and phrases to make your writing come alive.

What's in a Story?

Writing down your family history is an excellent way to turn memories into an engaging story. To fill out your tale, consider using some of the questions that newspapers answer in their articles:

1. Who?
- Who was involved in the story you are telling?
- Was it a person or an animal or maybe even a doll?
- Were you alone or was there a group of people? Who was active and who just observed?
- Include details: When you describe who is in the story, your words come alive so your reader can imagine being right there, too.

2. What?
- What is the main event you're describing?
- Do you need some background information (so the reader understands why you were late for school, for example)?

- Describe what happened in a sequence that gives shape to the story: what were you (or the main characters) doing when the story began? Go through the events to paint a complete picture of what happened.

3. Where?
- Where did the event happen? Give enough details so the reader can picture the setting.
- What was the importance of the location to your story?
- What did the place look like and feel like? If you were young and at school, you may need to describe how spooky the school was with no other kids around.

4. When?
- When did the story happen? If appropriate, include details like what kind of cars people were driving and what clothes they wore.
- Don't assume your readers will know what the Midwest looked like in the 1950s (or even last Christmas). Describe it in detail. When something happened may be as important as the event itself.

5. Why?
- Why was this story important to you or the person you interviewed?
- What did you/they learn from it?
- Explain what the experience meant to you or to

your subject. Did it change the way you/they looked at things?

Pulling the Story Together

Once you have gathered all the information, either from your interviews or from your own reminiscences, you can begin to pull the story together. Whether you are writing a biographical or autobiographical story, try to stick to the facts. At some point you may want to write a fictional story, but at this stage you'll want to be as accurate and truthful as possible.

Consider the material you have gathered and determine in what sequence to present it. Once you have written your first draft, it will be easier to see where you need to add more material and where some can be tightened. You can also get clarification regarding any points that are ambiguous. For example, you may need to briefly re-interview your source about something that needs to be explained further. For your own stories, it may help to corroborate missing information with someone who was there or knows about the details you are seeking. Never be afraid of making your stories as historically factual as you can.

Writing Journal

When starting a family history, I find it really useful to keep a writing journal. In fact, it may be one of the very best tools you will ever use. It can be any kind of a notebook or even a stack of paper, as long as you can keep your pieces of writing together. It doesn't have to be anything fancy, but some writers like to use beautiful journals, perhaps with a theme or picture on the cover that inspires them.

When you happen to think of some vivid memories or pleasing words, write them down in your journal to help you develop your "writer's eye." Even a little snippet or two is good. Just jot down things as you think of them. When you are ready to write a story, scan through your journal for some writing inspiration. It will remind you of things you have seen or recalled.

So What's in a Writing Journal?

What you put in your writing journal will be as unique to you as how you pack your suitcase for a trip. Use it as a place to save bits and pieces and words that appeal to you, things you don't want to forget, such as phrases and images, fragment of conversation and anything else that grabs your attention. Your journal can have anything in it you want, including drawings, sketches, and pictures.

Some writers use more than one writing journal at a time. For example, I might have one for my own family stories, another for recipes, and a third for magazine article ideas. I always keep a tablet in my car and one in my purse so I don't lose those lovely thoughts and ideas that pop into my mind at unpredictable times. Some of my best inspirations have occurred when least expected and I don't want to lose them.

Alternative Considerations for Family Stories

Many people, including most kids, are technically savvy these days, which allows for several interesting alternative ways to publish your family stories. In addition to a printed version of your personal history, or instead of, consider choosing other options that may enhance your family story experience.

You can enter your stories into a word processing application, such as Microsoft Word, which has the added advantage of an automated spelling checker. You can also store information on your own website, on a Web log (blog) or on a commercial website that allows multiple people to enter information from anywhere in the world. An added bonus of using newer technology is that it will appeal greatly to computer-literate kids and grandkids. If you are less knowledgeable technically, let the younger generations show you how to use it. This is a win-win situation when they can share their expertise with you.

The hardest part of almost any project is getting started. My mom and I enjoyed wallpapering rooms together. Whenever we finished hanging the very first sheet of wallpaper, she always stepped back, took a close look, and said, "There. Now we're halfway done." Naturally, we were nowhere near being halfway finished. But we did a great deal of prep work before getting even that far, so it really did feel like we accomplished something significant. After that, the rest of the job was easy!

So how do you start writing your family stories? The easiest way is to scribble down a few sentences about something that you remember from an earlier time. It doesn't have to be anything long and tedious. The important thing is to have fun and get something down on paper. No writer expects her first words to be the final version and neither should you. Take a few minutes to recall a memory and jot down a handful of details. Now you are "halfway done."

How Do You Eat an Elephant?

Did you ever hear the riddle about how you eat an elephant? Simple. You eat it one bite at a time! Pretty much like you'd eat a slice of chocolate cake, right? Writing a story is the same way—you just start with one idea at a time. Don't worry about how everything is going to fit together at the end. Take one small piece and build it up bite by bite.

By the same token, any journey begins with one small step. Take that step today and soon you will be on the road to gathering family stories about the important people in your life.

First Bite—the Title

Start by writing down a title for each story. The title is

the heart of your story. You can always change it later, but having a title in front of you helps to focus on one topic. Once you select a title, consider how you want the story to flow. The most straightforward method is to keep events in a chronological order, but at some point you may choose to vary the sequence.

Second Bite—the Introduction

Think about the story you want to tell. You need to organize your thoughts for it to make sense to you as you write and to your readers when you are finished. The beginning paragraph is the introduction to the story. Use it to grab your reader's attention and make them want to read more.

By using vivid imagery, you can draw in readers from the very first paragraph. They will become curious to know more about the rest of the story.

Third Bite—the Details

The middle paragraphs hold the details of your story. Each paragraph should be about one portion of the tale. Some of them may be short, some longer. Keep in mind that a really long paragraph may be hard to follow, in which case it helps to break it up. Reading your story aloud helps you hear how well it makes sense.

When you start telling the next part of your story, that is probably a good time for a new paragraph. To decide if a paragraph should be a continuation of the previous one, consider the main idea in each of them. Each new topic calls for a new paragraph.

Fourth Bite—the Ending

The ending paragraph wraps up the story. It is an ideal place to summarize the point of your story and to leave your reader with a thought of "Oh, I see how it was." They feel satisfied that your story didn't leave any loose ends hanging.

♥

PART FOUR: GOING FORWARD

From Your Heart to Their Hands

♥

Chapter Eleven: Preserving Your Legacy Letter

Planning for Forever and Ever Amen

"Many people wrongly assume that the most important issue among families is money and wealth transfer—it's not. What we found was the memories, the stories, the values were ten times more important to people than the money."

~ Ken Dychtwald, American psychologist, gerontologist, documentary filmmaker, and entrepreneur

Once you've completed each of the above exercises, congratulate yourself! You are almost finished. You will now create your own legacy letter. Keep in mind that each person's document will be uniquely personal—no two will be alike.

1. For each of the six sections, create a page or two (or perhaps more or less) in a way that expresses what you want to convey to your family and friends. It may help to write as if you are speaking to a specific person. Often, it is easier

75

to address your innermost thoughts on paper than it is face to face.

2. When you are comfortable with your message, write or print it onto archival paper, which is a special type of paper that is designed to not yellow or deteriorate with age; it is available in a variety of colors and patterns at office supply stores and craft stores.

3. Upon completion of your legacy letter, sit back and reflect on a job well done!

Going forward, enjoy the satisfaction of having completed your legacy letter. You have accomplished an important step for yourself and others. We strongly recommend you share it in the near future with your loved ones, which provides you an opportunity to enhance your relationship with your family and friends, as well as open new lines of communication.

If you decide to save your legacy letter until a later date, make sure you leave specific instructions for its dissemination.

1. Store your original legacy letter in a secure place with instructions on who should see it and when. Keep each letter sealed in a pretty envelope with the recipient's name on the front. Whether you keep it at home or in a safety deposit box at a

bank, ensure it will be available at the time you designate.

2. Keep a copy of your legacy letter available at home as a source of inspiration for yourself in the future. You may also choose to transfer your legacy letter to an electronic format, such as into a word processor, audio recording, or video recording. Regardless of the format, always make an extra copy for safekeeping. Check out Appendix A for the pros and cons of various media for your legacy letter.

3. At a later date, you may discover more information to include in your legacy letter. That is wonderful. You can modify or add to it at any time at your discretion. You may also decide to share it with other people, such as new members of your family.

4. Updating your legacy letter on a regular basis, such as every few years, allows you to see how you have grown and changed over the years, as well as how life has impacted you.

5. Another ideal time to update your legacy letter is before or after milestone events, such as births, deaths, marriage, divorce, graduations, accomplishments, serious illness, or any other situations that are important to you.

Here is one last suggestion for delivering your legacy letter. Have someone read it aloud as a eulogy at your memorial service or funeral. You will have the final word to your friends and family, which will give them something special to remember you by.

Find peace of mind

by leaving a piece of your mind.

APPENDICES

♥

Appendix A – Legacy Letter Media Pros and Cons

The final format you decide to use for your legacy letter is up to you. There are many options available, from a simple paper letter to any number of imaginative expressions from your heart. Feel free to find the ones that are most comfortable for you.

Here are several options to consider for your legacy letter:

1. **Handwritten on archival paper:**
   - Pros: Handwriting is more personal; long-term retention
   - Cons: May be difficult to decipher

2. **Keyed into a Word Processor and printed on archival paper:**
   - Pros: Easy to make multiple copies; long-term retention
   - Cons: Requires some computer skills; storage media becomes obsolete

3. **Digital audio recording:**
   - Pros: Captures your voice; easy to make copies
   - Cons: No visual image; storage media becomes obsolete

4. **Video recording:**
   - Pros: Preserves your voice and image; easy to make copies
   - Cons: Potential camera awkwardness; storage media becomes obsolete

5. **Creative expressions:**
   - Examples: a painting, scrapbook, woodworking, embroidery, sculpture, quilt
   - Pros: Unique
   - Cons: Interpretation of the meaning may not be obvious. Consider including or attaching a short note that explains the significance of the unique piece you are leaving for posterity.

Appendix B – Sample Legacy Letters

From Linda L.:

To My Perfect Children and to All Who I Love,

As I write this letter my journey through life is not yet over, but it is getting toward the end. It is not at all scary to be here and it's kind of fun to look back. When I think about it, Life kind of falls into chapters, and each chapter is a lesson of sorts. Your journey and your Life's Lessons will be different than mine, but I believe that part of who we become is passed on from those who came before us, often subtly and without intent.

Many of my beliefs and values are rooted in the lessons I learned while growing up in the Humboldt Park neighborhood of Chicago during the 1940s and 1950s. The neighborhood was in constant flux during those years and people from many different countries and cultures came and went through my life. I learned to respect other people's beliefs and traditions, even though they are often different from my own.

I am grateful for the tapestry of life that God has given me. You, my children, have always been my best blessing of all. I am very proud of the life that each of you live, and the person that each of you has become. I like to think that much of who you are came through me ... even though I know that ultimately, we all make our own choices in life, and that is who we are.

With All My Love,

Mom

From Barbara Corn Ort:

A Life Lesson for Everyone I Have Been Lucky to Love

Every day...

Say "thank you." Smile. Hug.

Remember to...

Listen deeply. Ponder the words spoken. Welcome unexpected occurrences.

Laugh at yourself.

Give love and receive love with enthusiasm!

From Jean Lambert Zack:

The 1930s and 40s, as a standard of comparison, were before:

- The Pill
- Antibiotics
- Polio vaccine
- frozen foods
- Nylon
- ball point pens (we filled our ink pens from an ink bottle at home, or the ink well on our desks at school)
- jewelry was worn only by women
- the American flag had 48 stars

- there were no automatic dish washers, washing machines or clothes dryers

We also had NO running hot water! Taking baths required heating a kettle of water on the stove. We three children took our Saturday baths in turns, all in the same water. The first one in came out with red skin and the last with blue skin and goose bumps.

From Debra K. Turrell:

Each of you has an amazing and miraculous God story all your own. Each of you were miraculously placed into our family at just the right time, and most of you traveled halfway around the world to do so. If that isn't God's hand on you, I am hard-pressed to find a more amazing example of God working in the lives of His children. I am humbled and privileged to call you my children, and I thank God every day that He has given us to each other to be a family. Who else has such an amazing story as you do? From difficult beginnings you have been brought to a new land and new family and given a new and exceedingly abundant life.

[...]

So now as we look forward to what the rest of your life may hold, be strong and courageous, trust in God and believe His promises. May you find work that you enjoy and work at it with all your might. May you discover and use the gifts God has given uniquely to you and may you develop them to the fullest. May you find contentment and joy in the life God has given you to live. And may you gain strength and confidence from knowing God will never leave or forsake you, but instead will be with you wherever you go.

All My Love,
Mom

From Cindy Kamp:

For My Sons,

I believe that an important part of living is enjoyment, taking in all of life's experiences and reveling in the thrill of being alive. I have always had an eye for beauty, be it a maiden hair fern, an antique dish, or a leather-bound book, and have tried to fill my life and our home with things that are lovely to look at and that bring pleasure. There will never be enough days in my life to exhaust the list of things I want to do and learn, and I have been fortunate to live in a time and place that allowed me to experience so much. Part of this, however, is simply having the eyes to see all the things around us that are really beautiful.

One of my struggles has been to slow down enough to really see the rose, to touch the baby's cheek, to listen to the thunderstorm. For me, my lust for living has sometimes been unchecked and has actually worked against my ability to really enjoy the day. Let's just call it a developmental area! (Your father certainly does.)

[...]

In closing, you boys both know that I love you very much. However, I don't think either of you can ever understand how lucky I felt when I married your father, and then, at the age of 40 welcomed you into the world, P., and at 41, you, B. Your births will always remain something of a miracle in my mind. You see, at 36 I was making my peace with a full, but to be honest, a rather lonely, single life. Now at 46 I still pinch myself to see the two of you, like little puppies together, laughing and playing and bringing more joy into my life than you could ever know.

You have each been born with a fine mind and a beautiful spirit, and I am enjoying watching the tapestry of your lives come together, thread by thread. Especially during your early baby days, the metaphor that came to mind over and over for me was that of watching the most exquisite rose I had ever seen unfold, petal by petal. You, and your father, will always be the most exquisite flowers in the garden of my life.

Your Mother,

Cindy

From Maria Williams:

My mother's life made me value self-reliance, being on time, and self-actualization. I have her DNA of being responsive (good or bad), nurturing and being a selfless mother. I hope these blessings provided you the inspiration to face those difficult times in your lives. Make no mistake. At times, I am also a bundle of contradiction when stressed or challenged. Deep inside I would say, "Don't tread on me!" and then I struggle for your understanding.

When my mother passed away, I often find myself asking for her forgiveness for my shortcomings, and I have plenty of them. Of late, I regret and feel sad that I did not keep any of her letters—cherished memories all gone.

Mom's death was painfully excruciating. I was alone with her at her hospital bed when her doctor told me to call the rest of the family to come to the hospital, for her end was near. Intense loneliness and sadness brought tears to my eyes. I am still surviving this rough spot of my life. My mother and I were emotionally distant. I was kept at the surface and was limited to penetrate the core of ways and byways of our family life. My attempts for closure with her did not materialize. However, I am very grateful for my sister for taking care of Mom's physical and emotional needs while she was alive.

From Ellen M. Smith:

Since we had both been raised rather poor (poor and poorer), I knew that I wanted to help the less fortunate. We retired with two pensions, two Social Security checks, and no bills. That's why we do so much volunteer work through visits, nursing homes, talking with friends about their problems, cooking for sick people and death in families, quilting, crocheting, or whatever come up. It takes a lot of my time, and in return I feel very rewarded.

We retired as secure as anyone can be, so I also have opportunities for fun like my 4th dog (3 in the past). I bake major amounts of Christmas cookies (5,000 last year) and deliver them around the country, town, and world (many by mail). Also, I keep busy by crocheting wedding afghans and baby afghans, and other items that come along.

My Six Word Memoir: Loved, Wife, Mother, Grandma, Christ, Fulfilled.

From an Anonymous Student:

Achievements and Accomplishments:

I seemed to have the ability from a small child to be able to organize and figure out how to do things. I always had plans and dreams in my mind of what and where I wanted to go. That has never changed. I have tried to make a positive change in something every day of my life, I never hit the pillow at night angry about something or someone even if it takes a brisk walk at night in any kind of weather, to think it out and put the event into "in-active storage." I talk with my "GOD" fully realizing not all people have the same definition of my God… discussing the wonders of the Universe he or she has provided; us humans sure haven't done the job no matter how hard we try. I've learned negativism seldom works, positives have much more effect.

Personal Values and Beliefs:

Look forward to what you do, enjoy it while doing it and most important when you look back be glad you did it. (Of course this only applies to the moral system I used throughout my life). If you feel you need to hide something you better not be doing it. I've learned much more from the mistakes I've made than from the things I got right the first time! Difficult decisions I format in advance so when the situation happens I don't have to ponder my response…it's set to go; (example – I come upon a car wreck that is burning and I'm the only one there).

Hopes for the Future:

Stay involved in doing things with my family and others. Have a daily schedule (however, less strenuous than in the past). Keep abreast of some of the more significant things happening in our world, my community and family. This enables me to take part in discussions with friends and family with some relevant new information. High risk adventures are treated with a "good scoop of caution," as I have become elderly, however, "plain vanilla existence" is not part of my vision of the future.

From Julie Hartman:

I learned from my mother to treat everyone you meet with respect and kindness. My mother treated a downtrodden person the same as the bank president. Social status meant little to her. She never stopped being curious about life and really cared about people.

From my dad I learned how to be responsible for the welfare of your family and always, always show up on time.

From my divorce from your dad, I learned how to stand on my own two feet, forgiveness and that asking for help is a strong thing to do.

What did I learn from you? I have learned the meaning of unconditional love, patience, gratitude and the importance of letting go.

[...]

Sometimes when I would think about the task of raising you by myself it became too scary. What I would often do is think—let's get through the next hour, then let's get through this day and luckily God blessed me with you guys. When God closes a door, he often leaves a window open. So thank you for helping me to find that open window.

From my heart to yours,

Love,

Mom

From Lois Lauer:

As I look to the future, I am ever-hopeful that we as a human race are evolving into a more respectful earth community in which we respect and love and honor the diversity among people (race, creed, gender, culture, etc.), the bio-diversity of the earth's life, and the diversity of the land itself.

[...]

I am hopeful that I will enjoy this journey for many years to come; that, for whatever duration, I will live each day with love and joy and hope, with a continuing commitment to make this world a brighter, healthier, and more loving community.

[...]

I also believe in being positive. I learned the "look on the brighter side" so well, that I've had to struggle to learn to recognize my full range of emotions. But I think the lesson has served me well. It's made me the optimistic hopeful person that I am. I believe we can choose our lives—although we cannot control all our circumstances—we can choose our reaction—we don't need to think like victims—we can choose, as Tasha Tudor (Fra Giovanni) would say, to "TAKE JOY, TAKE PEACE, AND TAKE HEAVEN …."

Appendix C - Resources

Website Resources

- Author's website for Beth LaMie, author, international speaker and personal historian, where you can sign up for a free monthly newsletter with tips on writing family stories: www.bethlamie.com
- Association of Personal Historians (APH), which offers an anthology of personal stories: http://www.personalhistorians.org/
- Story of My Life.com. Free private website to accumulate all your family stories and invite participation from around the world. www.storyofmylife.com

Book Resources

- LaMie, Beth, *Granny's Guide to Writing Your Family Stories, For Kids from 8 to 98.* Solon, IA: Little Duck Publishing, 2010.
- LaMie, Beth, *Legacy Letters from Your Heart: How to Find Peace of Mind by Leaving a Piece of Your Mind.* Solon, IA: Little Duck Publishing, 2016.

- Goldberg, Natalie, *Writing Down the Bones.* Boston: Shambhala Publications, 1986.
- Greene, Bob, and Fulford, D.G., *To Our Children's Children, Preserving Family Histories for Generations to Come.* NY: Doubleday, 1993.
- LaMott, Anne, *Bird by Bird, Some Instructions on Writing and Life.* NY: Random House, 1995.
- Yost, Paula Stallings, and McNees, Pat, Eds. *My Words Are Gonna Linger, The Art of Personal History.* Kennebunk, Maine: Personal History Press, 2009.

ACKNOWLEDGMENTS

To my husband, Lynn, thank you for your ongoing support and patience. You are my best friend—my laptop is only number two.

To Barbara Sher, your inspiration and encouragement continue to be instrumental in achieving my dreams.

To the gracious members of my writing classes, thank you for sharing your own legacy letters for this book.

To all my readers, start writing a legacy letter today so your precious life stories and wisdom will not be lost.

Space for notes or writing journal entries

Space for notes or writing journal entries:

Space for notes or writing journal entries:

Space for notes or writing journal entries:

Space for notes or writing journal entries:

Space for notes or writing journal entries:

Space for notes or writing journal entries:

Space for notes or writing journal entries:

Space for notes or writing journal entries:

www.ingramcontent.com/pod-product-compliance
Lightning Source LLC
Chambersburg PA
CBHW072240290326
41934CB00008BB/1360